The Worship Leader's Guide to
CALLING ON GOD

Inclusive Christian Prayers for
Three Years of Sundays

Peter Bankson & Deborah Sokolove

Other Prayer and Worship Resources from SkyLight Paths

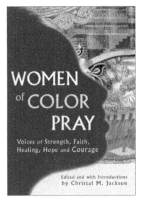

Women of Color Pray
Voices of Strength, Faith, Healing, Hope and Courage

Edited and with Introductions by Christal M. Jackson

This beautiful collection of prayers will take you on a journey into the spiritual walk of women of color around the world—including Asia, the Middle East and Africa—as well as Native American, African American, Asian American and Hispanic women in the United States.

5 x 7¼, 208 pp, Paperback, 978-1-59473-077-1

Men Pray
Voices of Strength, Faith, Healing, Hope and Courage
By the Editors at SkyLight Paths
Introductions by Brian D. McLaren
This collection celebrates the profound variety of ways men around the world have called out to the Divine—with words of joy, praise, gratitude, wonder, petition and even anger.

5 x 7¼, 192 pp, Hardcover, 978-1-59473-395-6

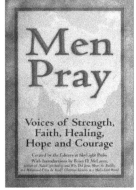

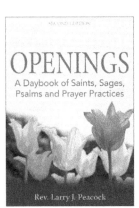

Openings, 2nd Edition
A Daybook of Saints, Sages, Psalms and Prayer Practices

By Rev. Larry J. Peacock

A prayerbook for every day of the year, with ancient and modern sages from inside and outside the Christian tradition and a wide variety of spiritual practices and reflections for every season.

6 x 9, 448 pp, Paperback, 978-1-59473-545-5

Sacred Attention
A Spiritual Practice for Finding God in the Moment
By Margaret D. McGee
Accessible, humorous and meaningful reflections and practices to help you deepen your awareness of yourself and your relationship to all that is around you—and within you.

6 x 9, 144 pp, Paperback, 978-1-59473-291-1; Hardcover, 978-1-59473-232-4

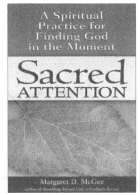

Praying with Our Hands
21 Practices of Embodied Prayer from the World's Spiritual Traditions

By Jon M. Sweeney
Photographs by Jennifer J. Wilson
Foreword by Mother Tessa Bielecki
Afterword by Taitetsu Unno, PhD

A spiritual guidebook for bringing prayer into our bodies, with twenty-one simple ways of using our hands to speak to God, presented in word and image.

8 x 8, 96 pp, 22 b/w photos, Paperback, 978-1-893361-16-4

Lectio Divina—The Sacred Art
Transforming Words & Images into Heart-Centered Prayer
By Christine Valters Paintner, PhD
Break open this ancient contemplative practice of listening deeply for God's voice in sacred texts—and expand your practice to include sacred reading of the world through image, sound, nature and life experience.

5½ x 8½, 240 pp, Paperback, 978-1-59473-300-0

CALLING ON GOD

Inclusive Christian Prayers for Three Years of Sundays

Worship Leader's Guide

Peter Bankson & Deborah Sokolove

CHRISTIAN JOURNEYS
FROM SKYLIGHT PATHS® PUBLISHING
Sunset Farm Offices, Route 4, P.O. Box 237, Woodstock, VT 05091
Tel: (802) 457-4000 Fax: (802) 457-40041
www.skylightpaths.com
www.christianjourneysbooks.com

Calling on God: Inclusive Christian Prayers for Three Years of Sundays—Worship Leader's Guide

2014 Paperback Edition, First Printing

For information regarding permission to reprint material from this book, please mail or fax your request in writing to SkyLight Paths Publishing, Permissions Department, at the address / fax number listed below, or email your request to permissions@skylightpaths.com.

10 9 8 7 6 5 4 3 2 1

Manufactured in the United States of America

Cover design: Michael Myers

Cover art: Deborah Sokolove

SkyLight Paths Publishing is creating a place where people of different spiritual traditions come together for challenge and inspiration, a place where we can help each other understand the mystery that lies at the heart of our existence.

SkyLight Paths sees both believers and seekers as a community that increasingly transcends traditional boundaries of religion and denomination—people wanting to learn from each other, *walking together, finding the way*.

SkyLight Paths, "Walking Together, Finding the Way" and colophon are trademarks of LongHill Partners, Inc., registered in the U.S. Patent and Trademark Office.

Walking Together, Finding the Way
Published by SkyLight Paths Publishing
A Division of LongHill Partners, Inc.
Sunset Farm Offices, Route 4, P.O. Box 237
Woodstock, VT 05091
Tel: (802) 457-4000 Fax: (802) 457-4004
www.skylightpaths.com

Contents

A Typical Order of
Service for Seekers Church

We hope the prayers in *Calling on God* are a blessing to you and your worshiping community. Below is an annotated basic order of worship for Seekers Church to give you an idea of how the prayers in *Calling on God* fit into our overall worship. Using this outline, Celebration Circle writes a new order of worship for each season.

GATHERING

An informal thirty-minute gathering outside the sanctuary provides an opportunity to share news, welcome visitors, celebrate birthdays, and make announcements about activities of interest to community members. At the conclusion of Gathering Time, a member offers a prayer for peace and justice, lights a candle, and leads the congregation upstairs to continue worship in the sanctuary.

Entrance

We enter the sanctuary in silence, to continue our worship with a time of reflection. There is a visual composition on the altar table beneath the life-sized empty cross. These images and the bulletin covers relate to the worship theme for the season. There is also a reading in the liturgy for silent reflection during this time. Like the composition on the altar, these readings nurture reflection on the worship theme for the season. This initial time for reflection includes music chosen to complement the sermon and members of the community lighting candles on the altar table. This is often an opportunity for our children to help lead us in worship.

Call to Worship

We open our worship with an invitation to bring ourselves—spirit, mind, and body—into the presence of God with a call to worship meant to remind all of us that we are among God's beloved, welcomed into the body of the risen Christ. Here is a sample Easter call to worship, written by the Celebration Circle:

Leader: Christ is risen!

People: Christ is risen indeed! Alleluia!

Leader: We come to retell the ancient stories,
to restore our dreams and hopes for new beginnings.

**People: We come with joy to laugh and sing,
to remember that love is stronger than death.**

Leader: We come to celebrate the power of resurrection,
  even when all hope seems lost.
  Christ is risen!

All: Christ is risen indeed! Alleluia!

Opening Prayer

The worship leader offers a version of the opening prayers in *Calling on God*.

Hymn

Word for the Children

The word for the children is based on the lectionary readings for the week and offered by a member of the informal group that coordinates our Sunday School.

Silence

The silence is normally at least two minutes; it is held by the worship leader.

PRAYERS

Common Confession and Assurance

The confession and assurance are written by Celebration Circle for the season. Following the initial prayer, the worship leader invites prayers from the congregation "aloud and in silence," and holds the space until there is a sense that all who wish to pray aloud have offered their prayers.

When it seems that no one else wants to pray aloud, the leader offers the assurance. Here is an example of a confession and assurance from the Easter season:

Leader: Holy One, even as we celebrate
  the resurrection of your chosen one,
  we remain skeptical.

**People: We confess that we often do not believe
  that we are newly born into living hope.**

Leader: We seek to live in the power
  of imagination, myth, and dreams.

**People: But usually we cling
  to what we see, know, and experience,
  afraid to trust the reality beyond our knowing.**

Leader: When goodness, beauty, and love
  seem too much to hope for,
  we forget to rely on your promised deliverance.

**All: Holy One, hear our prayers, forgive us,
and restore us to the joy of your salvation.**

(allow time for congregants to pray aloud)

Leader: In the risen Christ,
God's mercy triumphs over sin and death.
Through Jesus's name we receive
forgiveness of all our sins.

All: Amen.

Prayers of Thanksgiving and Intercession

Following the prayers of confession and assurance, the worship leader offers an introductory prayer that speaks of situations throughout the world, the community, and within the congregation for which to give thanks and praise to God. This bidding prayer invites further prayers of thanksgiving and praise from the congregation.

When there is a sense that all who wish to pray aloud have done so, the worship leader offers another bidding prayer inviting the congregation into a time of petition and intercession. These prayers inviting the congregation's participation are found in *Calling on God*.

Prayer of Commitment

When the congregation falls silent after the prayers of thanksgiving and intercession, the worship leader may say something like, "Gathering all of our prayers into one, let us join in the prayer of commitment." The following community prayer is inspired by the Lord's Prayer and the members' commitment statement of Seekers Church:

O Holy One, we come today
to claim our relationship with you.

We pray for the commitment to grow together,
sharing the gifts you give us with others
here and in the wider world.

Forgive us for the hurt we have inflicted,
and help us forgive those who have hurt us.

Give us strength and discipline
to nurture our relationship with you;
to care for every part of your creation;
to foster justice and be in solidarity with those in need;
to work to end all war, and violence, and discord;
and to respond joyfully when you call,
freely giving ourselves as you have shown the way.

We open our hearts to you and your creation
in the name of Jesus, who is the Christ. Amen.

Hymn

THE WORD

Scripture

The reading of the lectionary scriptures for the week is offered by different members of the community.

Sermon

The sermon is offered by a different individual (or group) each week, and is based on the lectionary scriptures for the week and the experience of the preacher.

Silent Reflection

The worship leader holds the silence as the congregation reflects on the sermon.

Offering

COMMUNION

We generally celebrate Communion on the first Sunday of every month, as well as on Easter Sunday. On those Sundays, a special order of worship is inserted into the worship folders. Most of the Communion liturgy remains the same from season to season, but the Great Thanksgiving portion, in which we give thanks to God for some aspect of the divine presence in creation, the life and work of Jesus, the action of the Holy Spirit, and for the church as the risen body of Christ, is written by Celebration Circle for each season.

Preparation

Leader 1: This is the table of the Heavenly Feast,
the joyful celebration of the people of God.

Leader 2: We gather now as one body, joined around the table.
Here we celebrate God's presence among us
united in Christ's spirit, broken and whole all at once.

**All: Nourished and hungry, loved and loving,
sinner and forgiven;
we make one circle of knowing,
believing, rejoicing, being,
as God lights and rests among us.**

Great Thanksgiving

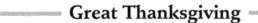

Leader 1: Holy Maker of living hope, we give you thanks for life,
for dreams and memories that help us stand together
in the face of grief and loss.

**All: We give you thanks for your Holy Spirit,
filling us with laughter
as we learn to live and love anew.**

Leader 2: We give you thanks for your Holy Child, Jesus,
 whose life and death and resurrection
 raise hope beyond experience.

All: We give you thanks for your holy church,
 with steady roots and open flowers of hope,
 calling us to be your body here and now,
 in new, surprising, hopeful ways.

Blessing the Elements

Leader 1: Christ invites everyone to eat the bread of life,
 to drink the cup of the new covenant.

Leader 2: Jesus said, *I am the bread of life.*
 You who come to me shall never hunger,
 You who believe in me shall never thirst.

Leader 1: On the night of his arrest, Jesus took bread,
 and after giving thanks to God, broke it and said,
 This is my body,
 broken for the healing of the world.
 Whenever you eat it, do so remembering me.

Leader 2: After supper, Jesus took the cup and said,
 This is the cup of the new covenant,
 poured out for you and for all.
 Whenever you drink it, do so remembering me.

All: O Holy One, send down your Spirit
 that these gifts of bread and cup
 may be for us the body and blood of Christ.
 Unite us with Christ forever
 and bring us with the whole creation
 to your eternal realm.

Share the Elements

If anyone does not wish to receive the elements, they are welcome to join the circle and allow the elements to pass, or remain in their seats. We serve grape juice in our cups.

Prayer of Thanksgiving and Dedication

All: God of abundance and mercy,
 we give joyful thanks
 for your eternal love and healing presence
 in our celebration of bread and cup.
 Bless this body of Christ
 that we may attend faithfully

to our call to be your servants,
with each other and throughout the world.
Amen.

RESPONDING IN FAITH

Shared Reflections

After Communion or the sermon, there is an opportunity for anyone present to offer their own reflections on the scripture lessons for the week or their response to worship.

Announcements

The worship leader invites members of the community to share announcements about events of interest to the community.

Hymn

Benediction

We close our worship with a blessing meant to remind all of us that we are among God's beloved, welcomed into the body of the risen Christ, and sent forth to respond to God's call to love and serve God's creation. The benedictions in the worship of Seekers Church are written by the Celebration Circle as part of the seasonal liturgy. We use the same benediction for the six to eight weeks of a liturgical season. Here is a sample Easter-season benediction, when the worship theme was "Living Hope":

> Leader: Let us go forth from this place
>   leaving the empty tomb behind.
>   Let us tell again the ancient saving stories
>   and celebrate the triumph of love over death,
>   hope over fear, joy over sadness.
>   Be the good news that Christ has risen indeed!
>
> **All: Alleluia! Amen.**

The Visual Environment for Worship

As Celebration Circle writes and edits prayers for the services, we also address the question of the visual environment. As you prepare for worship each Sunday, we encourage you to consider how the language of the prayers might be enhanced through artwork, lighting, and meaningful arrangements of various objects.

At Seekers Church, we print copies of the order of worship for all the Sundays of a given season. The covers for these bulletins are imaginatively designed to complement the liturgical theme, and are made by Celebration Circle or other members of the congregation. Original artwork by adults or children is frequently used and kept for reuse in subsequent years. Sometimes this artwork is created by a single individual; other times it is the result of a communal exercise in collaborative art making. In either case the bulletin covers are a strong visual and tactile reminder of the values of creative energy and interdependence held by this community.

While it is sometimes altered for special events, the arrangement of the worship room remains substantially the same from week to week and season to season—the chairs form a rough semicircle, leaving an aisle from the central entrance doors to the altar table. A rough-hewn wooden cross—made especially for the space by a member of Seekers Church from a cherry tree that had been cut down in the yard of another member—hangs on a curved wooden partition wall. There is also an altar table and a small wooden lectern made from cherry wood in the same style as the cross. Other than windows on the walls adjacent to the cross and a net to which people sometimes attach small photographs or other objects symbolizing situations needing prayer, the second-floor room is very plain.

A processional cross and congregational banner made by other members of the community are usually present somewhere in the room as well, but the table with the cross above it is the primary visual focus during worship. As a way of both symbolically and literally laying our lives at the foot of the cross, the table may hold anything from boxing gloves to artists' manikins or a basket of summer fruit in addition to the usual candles and Communion elements. Sometimes fabric, flowers, or other objects also hang from the ceiling, fill the windowsills, or are attached to the cross, creating a visual environment that embraces the entire congregation.

As we do with the textual portion of the liturgy, the members of Celebration Circle brainstorm to arrive at images and symbols to be used as a visual analogue to the words of the liturgy. We work with the theme for the season, the portions of the text already written, and go back to the lectionary readings for inspiration. Sometimes one person will have a flash of insight and others will add details until everyone feels that it is "right." Much of this conversation is theological, as we wrestle with the implications and nuances of textures, shapes, colors, and objects.

Once the basic elements of the visual arrangement are decided, we delegate one or two people to obtain or make what is needed. Because our worship space is used for many different events by many groups, all the parts are assembled before worship each Sunday and afterward put away for the next week. Sometimes some detail is deliberately changed from week to week, but even when this is not so, the visual environment looks a little different each time than it did the week before. While often one person takes on the main responsibility for these temporary art installations, others make suggestions or changes.

While there are no limits to imagination, there are some considerations that need to be taken into account when designing seasonal additions to the visual environment. For instance, objects on or near the altar need to be large enough to be seen from the back row, but not so large that they get in the way of those who are leading worship or obscure the Communion elements or other items that are important to the particular congregation. The shape of the room will also affect how things are perceived—in a long, narrow room, everything will be seen from the same angle, while in a wide room or where worship is in the round, the installation needs to make sense from multiple viewing angles.

Generally speaking, simple is best, unless what you want to convey is a sense of clutter. We often try to maintain continuity from one season to the next, sometimes carrying elements from Lent over into the Easter season but changing them in some way. Alternatively, making a radical change at the start of a new season signals to the congregation that something is different even before a single word is spoken.

One of the things that makes our work a little easier is that we have an extensive "prop closet"—a storage room with many different kinds of fabric, candle holders, baskets, rocks, and many other odd things that we have collected over time. We also look for suitable items at home, scour thrift shops and craft stores, and bring things home from our travels that find their way into the worship space at one time or another. It also helps to have a budget, because often the image or idea that you want to convey requires a specific color of fabric that you don't happen to have, or some other item that none of you ever thought of before.

The main ingredients, however, are a lively imagination, a willingness to try anything, and a reasonably good sense of design. After all, whatever you do, it's only for a season. In a few weeks you get to do something else entirely new.

CREATING LITURGIES COLLABORATIVELY

The liturgies used at Seekers Church are created anew each season by a small group called Celebration Circle, which guides and organizes our worship. Numbering at any given time from three to seven members, Celebration Circle is part accountability group and part committee. It is one of several mission groups that serve as places of deeper belonging, in which church members live out their commitments to mission as an expression of their outward journey; to the communal life of the church; and to spiritual growth, or the inward journey.

Celebration Circle is committed to deep personal sharing, mutual trust, and collaboration as the method by which it approaches its work. Celebration Circle meets weekly for two hours. Each meeting includes a brief time for worship followed by personal sharing, the exchange of written spiritual reports, coordinating the details of upcoming worship and working on the liturgy for the next season.

OUR COLLABORATIVE PROCESS

In order to maintain a flexible but familiar framework for the worship of the community, Celebration Circle is committed to collaboration as a guiding principle. In practice, this collaboration may take many forms and occurs on many different levels. A typical sequence is as follows:

Several times a year, we think together about themes for the coming seasons. All members of the group read the lections for each of the seasons to be considered, in order both to familiarize themselves with the texts and to find some common image or idea to give focus to the season. At the next meeting, the images and ideas are shared and discussed and new ideas grow out of a brainstorming process in which no thought is rejected as being too silly or disrespectful. These sessions often are marked by playful high spirits and laughter, alternating with somber moments when we are touched at a deep level. Eventually, there is a moment when we hear as one, when it is apparent that not only the theme but the words have been found to express the way that this year's Advent, for instance, differs from any other year's. Generally we work on a single season at a time. However, sometimes the themes for an entire festal cycle—such as the period that begins with Advent and ends with the Feast of the Epiphany, or the one that begins with Ash Wednesday and carries through Lent and Easter until the Feast of Pentecost—may emerge in one session.

Once the theme for a season has been found, we look for a short reading as a meditative focus. Referred to as a "reflection paragraph," this short piece of poetry or other excerpt from theological, spiritual, or devotional writings appears at the beginning of the seasonal worship bulletin. As group members read their suggestions aloud, ideas are generated for other parts of the liturgy. Sometimes, there is disagreement, suggestions for editorial changes, or even a consensus that we need to keep looking and come back the following week with new ideas. More often, however, the right reflection paragraph seems obvious to everyone, as if the Holy Spirit has been whispering in all our ears.

At this point, a number of different things may happen. Very occasionally, one person may be inspired to write the entire liturgy based on all the ideas and images that have emerged in the conversations on theme and will bring it to the group for comments and suggestions. Generally, however, various individuals volunteer to write one or more sections and bring them back to the next meeting. Liturgies written for the current season in other years are sometimes consulted, and occasionally a section or two, or even an entire liturgy, will be reused as is, or with some minor modification. As is true for the reflection paragraph, ideas for liturgy may come from a variety of sources, including hymn texts, denominational books of worship, time-honored prayers of the church universal, inspirational writings from other traditions, or the original writings of members of the community.

When the various parts of the liturgy are written, they are printed out in the proper order and read aloud, one person taking the part of the leader and the others that of the congregation. This allows us to hear any clumsiness of language, find any tongue-twisters, and discuss the finer theological points of one phrasing or another. If there is enough time, there may be two or more read-throughs in successive weeks, allowing for further refinements of both language and typography.

COLLABORATION AND THEOLOGY

Collaboration is the practical working out of a theology in which the definition of the priesthood of all believers includes such concepts as shared leadership, Christian servanthood, and authority at the point of one's gift. This is a very demanding way of working. For those who are used to writing or art making as a solitary endeavor—the outpouring of an individual intellect and soul—it is a discipline that takes some getting used to. Collaboration requires putting one's best efforts at the service of the group and a willingness to let go of those best efforts when it is clear that something else is needed.

The difference between collaboration and creation by committee is not unlike that between *sense of the meeting*, as it is practiced by the Religious Society of Friends (Quakers), and *consensus* as it is practiced in many secular organizations. In Barry Morely's booklet "Beyond Consensus," he discusses how decisions are made among Quakers as they come to agree on the "sense of the meeting." He says that consensus

> is achieved through a process of reasoning in which reasonable people search for a satisfactory decision.... Through consensus we decide it; through sense of the meeting we turn it over, allowing it to be decided. "Reaching consensus is a secular process," says a Friend. "In sense of the meeting God gets a voice."[1]

Similarly, whether writing liturgy or designing the visual environment or deciding on the image for the bulletin cover, the members of Celebration Circle do not seek to impose their wills upon one another or to convince one another of the rightness of their idea. We do not automatically assume that the person with specialized training or talent in poetry, music, or art will have

---

1. Barry Morley, "Beyond Consensus: Salvaging Sense of the Meeting," Pendle Hill Pamphlet 307 (Wallingford PA: Pendle Hill Publications, 1993), 5.

the best solution. We do assume that those with specialized training or talent will put their gifts at the service of all, and often it is the case that a person with particular skills will offer to make something that has been envisioned by another. Our collaboration includes not only one another, but God.

It is deeply humbling to work in this way. When collaboration works—as it does surprisingly often—we are aware of the presence of the Holy Spirit in our midst, of God's gift of grace in our common life. It is this gift that we offer back into the larger community as the weekly liturgy—the work of the people.

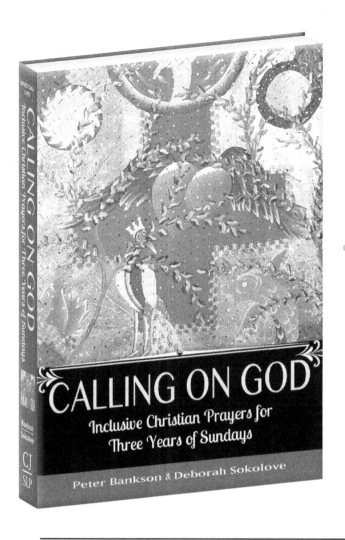 

Peter Bankson and **Deborah Sokolove** have been guiding people to connect with God in authentic, soul-satisfying ways for many years in their roles at Seekers Church in Washington, DC.

Peter Bankson has been a popular preacher, regular presider at worship and spiritual guide for Seekers Church since the mid-1980s. Formerly a colonel in the U.S. Army, he is now a member of the Servant Leadership Team and the mission groups that support worship and the ministry of place. He also experiments as a fiber sculptor, combining mathematical equations and sculptural crochet.

Deborah Sokolove writes and teaches on the relationship between the arts, culture and religious traditions. She is director of the Henry Luce III Center for the Arts and Religion at Wesley Theological Seminary, where she also serves as professor of art and worship. She is the author of *Sanctifying Art: Inviting Conversation between Artists, Theologians, and the Church* and has contributed articles to *Image, Call to Worship* and *The Arts in Religious and Theological Studies*. Her paintings have been shown around the country, appearing in many collections. Within Seekers Church, she serves on the worship planning group, frequently preaching and leading worship.

Other Leadership Resources from SkyLight Paths

Change and Conflict in Your Congregation (Even If You Hate Both)
How to Implement Conscious Choices, Manage Emotions and Build a Thriving Christian Community
By Rev. Anita L. Bradshaw, PhD
Positive, relational strategies and theological perspectives for navigating change and channeling conflict into a stronger sense of community and deeper understanding of one another.
6 x 9, 200 pp (est), Paperback, 978-1-59473-578-3

She Lives! *Sophia Wisdom Works in the World*
By Rev. Jann Aldredge-Clanton, PhD
Fascinating narratives of clergy and laypeople who are restoring sacred value to women and girls through Divine Feminine language and imagery in pursuit of just and equal faith communities.
6 x 9, 320 pp, Paperback, 978-1-59473-573-8

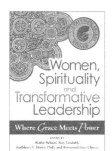

Women, Spirituality and Transformative Leadership: *Where Grace Meets Power*
Edited by Kathe Schaaf, Kay Lindahl, Kathleen S. Hurty, PhD, and Rev. Guo Cheen
Inspiring visions of personal leadership and powerful collaborative action. Explores the challenges and opportunities on the frontier of women's spiritual leadership.
6 x 9, 288 pp, Paperback, 978-1-59473-548-6

Learning to Lead: *Lessons in Leadership for People of Faith*
Edited by Rev. Willard W. C. Ashley Sr., MDiv, DMin, DH
Tools, advice, practical methodologies and case studies on how to help clergy and laypeople learn to do theology in context and grow into faith leadership roles.
6 x 9, 384 pp, Hardcover, 978-1-59473-432-8

CHRISTIAN JOURNEYS
FROM SKYLIGHT PATHS® PUBLISHING
Sunset Farm Offices, Route 4, P.O. Box 237, Woodstock, VT 05091
Tel: (802) 457-4000 Fax: (802) 457-40041
www.skylightpaths.com
www.christianjourneysbooks.com

Insights and Ideas for Planning Worship Using *Calling on God*

A guide to using *Calling on God* in worship communities, with:

- A sample order of service
- Suggestions for enhancing the visual environment for worship
- Guidelines for creating liturgies collaboratively in your own worship community

About *Calling on God: Inclusive Christian Prayers for Three Years of Sundays*

This special prayerbook is for today's Christians who find comfort in the rhythm of the traditional lectionary but long to connect with God in ways that are satisfying to the modern heart and mind. Founded on creativity, inclusivity and sharing, it encourages us to remember the divine elements of the natural world around us as we express our hopes and fears for others and ourselves. Inspiring words help us give thanks for human inventions and lament the evils of poverty, violence and oppression of all kinds while remaining mindful of God's promises of healing for a broken world.

Following the annual procession of the seasons with prayers that are appropriate for personal devotion as well as for use in leading worship, these new ways to call on God will feed your soul and inspire you to find your own fresh language for thanksgiving, praise, intercession and petition, whether in your community or personal spiritual life.

Praise for *Calling on God: Inclusive Christian Prayers for Three Years of Sundays*

"Beautiful, fresh language for Christians of all denominations.... These prayers can enrich our worship, transforming our hearts and—ultimately—strengthening our world."
— **Rev. Canon Jan Naylor Cope**, vicar, Washington National Cathedral

"Beautifully written.... An inspiring gift to all those who gather weekly to shape and sustain themselves as God's faithful people."
— **Rev. Wesley Granberg-Michaelson**, general secretary emeritus, Reformed Church in America

"In plain but powerful words, [this book] says exactly just what we all would want to say to God."
— **Bishop Eugene Taylor Sutton**, Episcopal Diocese of Maryland

"[A] rich collection.... Bring[s] human need before God in a poignant and compassionate way. Growing out of the life of one church, this book will bless many."
— **Ruth Duck, ThD**, professor of worship, Garrett-Evangelical Theological Seminary

"A powerful, prayerful, extremely useful worship aid [for] progressive congregations of many denominations and small-base communities alike.... Browse the table of contents when you need just the right prayer for many occasions."
— **Diann L. Neu**, cofounder and codirector of the Women's Alliance for Theology, Ethics and Ritual (WATER); coeditor, *New Feminist Christianity: Many Voices, Many Views*

CHRISTIAN JOURNEYS

FROM SKYLIGHT PATHS® PUBLISHING
Woodstock, Vermont
www.skylightpaths.com
www.christianjourneysbooks.com

Printed in the USA
CPSIA information can be obtained
at www.ICGtesting.com
JSHW060056150824
68134JS00032B/2753

OPENINGS

The Complete Leader's Guide to *Openings*, 2nd Edition:
A Daybook of Saints, Sages, Psalms and Prayer Practices

Rev. Larry J. Peacock

Other Resources for Retreats and Spiritual Growth Groups from SkyLight Paths

The Heartbeat of God
Finding the Sacred in the Middle of Everything

By Katharine Jefferts Schori; Foreword by Joan Chittister, OSB

The presiding bishop of the Episcopal Church explores our human connections—with each other, with other nations, with the whole of our environment—and the intersections of faith with issues like poverty, climate change, the economy and healthcare.

6 x 9, 240 pp, HC, 978-1-59473-292-8

The Heartbeat of God Leader's Guide
By Jenifer Gamber
8½ x 11, 83 pp, PB, 978-1-59473-308-6

Sacred Attention
A Spiritual Practice for Finding God in the Moment
By Margaret D. McGee

Accessible, humorous and meaningful reflections and practices to help you deepen your awareness of yourself and your relationship to all that is around you—and within you.

6 x 9, 144 pp, Quality PB, 978-1-59473-291-1; HC, 978-1-59473-232-4

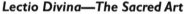

Lectio Divina—The Sacred Art
Transforming Words & Images into Heart-Centered Prayer

By Christine Valters Paintner, PhD

Break open this ancient contemplative practice of listening deeply for the Divine in sacred texts as well as in images, sounds, nature and all of life's experiences.

5½ x 8½, 240 pp, Quality PB Original, 978-1-59473-300-0

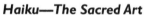

Haiku—The Sacred Art
A Spiritual Practice in Three Lines
By Margaret D. McGee

Introduces haiku as a simple and effective way of tapping into the sacred moments that permeate everyday living.

5½ x 8½, 192 pp, Quality PB Original, 978-1-59473-269-0

Finding Hope
Cultivating God's Gift of a Hopeful Spirit

By Marcia Ford; Foreword by Andrea Jaeger

Provides important learning tools that you can apply to everyday life experiences, inspiring personal stories of hope from the famous and not-so-famous, and realistic exercises for creating the overall balance and peace you look to achieve in living your life connected to God.

8 x 8, 176 pp, Quality PB Original, 978-1-59473-211-9

Dance—The Sacred Art
The Joy of Movement as a Spiritual Practice
By Cynthia Winton-Henry

Helps you overcome embarrassment or anxiety and discover in dance a place of solace and restoration, as well as an energizing spiritual force.

5½ x 8½, 224 pp, Quality PB Original, 978-1-59473-268-3

Fully Awake and Truly Alive
Spiritual Practices to Nurture Your Soul

By Rev. Jane E. Vennard; Foreword by Rami Shapiro

With stories from her personal life and her experience as a spiritual director, Rev. Jane Vennard illustrates the joys and frustrations of spiritual practice. Includes insights from various religious traditions and exercises and meditations for your journey.

6 x 9, 208 pp, Quality PB Original, 978-1-59473-473-1

Soul Fire
Accessing Your Creativity
By Thomas Ryan, CSP

Shows you how to cultivate your creative spirit, particularly in the second half of life, as a way to encourage personal growth, enrich your spiritual life, and deepen your communion with God.

6 x 9, 160 pp, Quality PB Original, 978-1-59473-243-0

OPENINGS

A Daybook of Saints, Sages, Psalms and Prayer Practices

Leader's Guide

Rev. Larry J. Peacock

Walking Together, Finding the Way®

SKYLIGHT PATHS®
PUBLISHING
Woodstock, Vermont

Openings: A Daybook of Saints, Sages, Psalms, and Prayer Practices—Leader's Guide

2014 Paperback Edition, First Printing

© 2014 by Larry James Peacock

10 9 8 7 6 5 4 3 2 1

Manufactured in the United States of America

Cover Design: Kelley Barton
Cover Art: ©iStockphot.com/mirefa, modified by Tim Holtz
Interior Design: Michael Myers

Walking Together, Finding the Way®
Published by SkyLight Paths Publishing
A Division of LongHill Partners, Inc.
Sunset Farm Offices, Route 4, P.O. Box 237
Woodstock, VT 05091
Tel: (802) 457-4000   Fax: (802) 457-4004
www.skylightpaths.com

Contents

Introduction

My hope is that using *Openings* will set in place a daily pattern of reflection and prayer, and open you to people of deep faith, generous compassion, and bold words and actions. I'd like it to give you a language for prayer from the Psalms, and help you discover a wonderful variety of ways to stay connected to the Holy One.

Openings can also provide you with tools and resources to use in small groups, spiritual retreats, or teaching settings. This guide will suggest some possible uses, but I hope you will make *Openings* part of your toolbox for nurturing others on the spiritual journey, so I encourage you to fashion other ways to use *Openings* with others and I invite you to let me know what you have tried. Be empowered to guide others.

Psalms, Prayer Practices, and Opening to God

A Retreat Model

This can be adapted for a one- or two-day retreat. Two days will give you more space to let the group experience and practice the suggestions.

Retreat Opening

A Time of Welcoming

Invite participants to share names and one piece of information about themselves, such as where they are from or what they do, or what drew them to the retreat.

Invite one-word prayers—each person says one word as he or she looks forward to the retreat.

A Word about Retreats to Share with Participants

It is important to take time for reflection, to set apart some time with God, to look back with gratitude, and to listen for next steps for the future. You can find more information on retreats in the entries for June 1–14.

Suggestions will be given in this retreat model for ways to pray during the time together. As you consider the suggestions, listen for God's invitation. Give yourself the freedom to follow the leading of the Spirit, even if it means not following the suggestions exactly.

At times of sharing, encourage participants to share as much as they are comfortable. Say something like, "May we covenant together to keep what is shared confidential, only to be part of this retreat."

Retreat Themes

The Psalms were the prayer book of the Hebrews and they can guide our prayer practices. We will consider three prayer practices from the Psalms using entries from *Openings* as guidance. (Let participants know at this point which sessions will focus on which themes.)

1. Be still and know that I am God—Psalm 46:10

April 13 has a meditation about "Be still and know." There are several ways to befriend silence and practice attentiveness to God in silence. One way is through the breath prayer. This is described in the entries for January 3–5 and 7–14. Use information from those pages to introduce the breath prayer and to practice sitting in silence. The Suggested Resources section at the back of *Openings* lists other books that can supplement the suggestions from the January entries.

April 20 has a suggestion for a prayer stretch that you might try before one of the sitting-in-silence practices. A Quaker friend told me the key to sitting in silence is to still the body and then still the mind. Moving the body in a gentle prayer stretch, then turning your attention to focused breathing, can bring inner readiness to pray.

2. How Long, O Lord? The Act of Lamenting

Walter Brueggemann's *The Message of the Psalms* contains information on three categories of Psalms—Orientation, Disorientation, and Reorientation. This is often helpful background information for teaching about praise and lament, our next prayer practice.

The entry for January 17 (Psalm 13) gives the structure for a lament, which is clearly one of the psalms of disorientation that Brueggemann describes in his book. Laments can either be for personal situations or for national and international concerns. I find it helpful to suggest writing both kinds of laments using the structure described on January 17. For the community laments, you could have groups work on a particular issue they are concerned about; sometimes working with others creates a more robust and vivid lament. Other personal or individual lament psalms are Psalm 13, 28, and 59. Community or corporate laments are Psalm 58, 79, and 94.

3. Praise and Thanks—Psalm 30:4

The entries for May 2–12 give many suggestions for developing gratitude as a spiritual practice. Keeping a gratitude list is a practice I often suggest when I lead retreats. I have a variation called "The Five Gratitudes," in which each morning I list five gratitudes that can include the day before as well as the new day.

Consider choosing several writing exercises from the ones suggested in the entries for May 2–12, such as writing to someone, writing short blessing prayers, and writing a prayer of thanks. You could also use an acrostic: using a word like "thanksgiving," invite a different prayer of gratitude for each letter of the word.

Offer the opportunity for participants to share their writing if they wish. Provide paper and stamps for the letters to be mailed to encourage follow-through.

Some of the poets mentioned in *Openings* have poems about praising God for many gifts of creation. Emily Dickinson (Sept. 30) and Mary Oliver (Apr. 22) are two beloved poets whose work may be worth incorporating into the retreat.

Rule of Life
Day Retreat

The entries for November 6–17 have guidance for forming a rule of life. These are some questions that could form an outline for a day retreat.

What daily prayer practices do you use? What are you drawn to; what beckons you?

Consider silent prayer, scripture reading/*lectio divina*, intercession, journaling, singing/chanting, coloring mandalas/art, prayer beads, movement, walking a labyrinth, bedtime prayers, mealtime graces, and gratitude prayers.

What could you commit to on a daily basis? Where would you practice these disciplines?

Consider your daily schedule and what might realistically fit into it as a regular practice. See "An Invitation" (pp. xviii–xix) for suggestions on setting up a daily practice and creating a sacred space for it.

What weekly practices could be part of your rule of life?

Worship is usually one practice, but weekly study, support, prayer, or service groups are others. See July 25–31 for suggestions on sabbath practices.

What monthly, yearly, or episodic events can you incorporate into your rule?

Consider spiritual direction, personal retreats, attending special art or lecture events, going on a pilgrimage, or participating in a non-geographical covenant community.

A Four-Week Class on Prayer Practices

Often it helps to do a short-term class during which you introduce a new theme and new practice each week as well as checking in to see how participants are doing with their spiritual practices. I find it is helpful to begin with a review of the previous week's theme and practice and then introduce the new theme and practice. The readings in *Openings* will give you the background you need to guide the participants. Here are four suggested prayer practices that are easy to teach and are a great benefit to people on the spiritual journey.

1. Practicing the Presence of God—February 3–8, 12–18
Invite the group to set up markers in their day—places, people, times, and objects—that call them to prayer.

2. Intercession—March 11–24, August 15–20
The March entries describe several intercession practices you can teach the group. The August pages introduce a simple and beautiful prayer of lovingkindness that can be shared for individual practice and also prayed as a group, pausing for silent prayer between each of the sections.

3. *Lectio Divina*—March 2–9
This four-fold pattern of reading and praying with scripture is described in March. Choose a passage from the Gospels and introduce the pattern. Suggest that participants try the reflection and repetition pattern during the week.

4. Befriending Silence—January 3–5, 7–14
Helping people become comfortable in silent meditation or prayer is a great gift. Most of us have minds that wander and lips that talk, which make it hard to pay attention to the quiet whisper of the Spirit. One way to help still the mind and focus the attention is through the breath prayer. The January entries give suggestions for this prayer practice.

Writing Prayers/ Poetry

Throughout *Openings*, including the beginning monthly prayers, I have offered many prayers, suggestions, and encouragement for writing prayers. I believe that the act of writing often reveals thoughts and feelings that lie hidden from our consciousness. Our words give expression to praise and lament, thanksgiving and confession. Encourage your class, family, or group to pick up a pen or use their computer to write. Anyone who would like to could share their writing, or participants may simply wish to share what they experienced in using writing as a prayer practice.

Try a prayer of thanksgiving.

Choose an address for God, one that is familiar or new to you, then choose words that are colorful, fresh, and alive to describe your reasons for thanks.

Try several blessing prayers using the same opening lines: "Blessed are you, God of Creation, for you have given us ..."

See how many blessing prayers you can write in three minutes. Don't worry about spelling.

Write a call to worship using short phrases.

You may wish to use Psalm 100 (July 25) as an example or these lines from a call to worship I wrote for a Martin Luther King Jr. worship service:

A call to compassion

A vision of community

A dream of justice

For all God's children.

A way of walking

Resisiting evil

Marching for good

Stirring the soul of a nation

Echoing deep within

Calling us to God's new reign.

Here are three themes that you could use:

Write an Easter call to worship with the theme of surprise and joy.

Write a call to worship for Earth Day with a theme of care for the earth.

Write a call to worship for Mother's or Father's Day with the theme of love and family.

Go outside and write down ten things you notice.

Choose some connecting verbs and shape a simple poem of creation.

Family Prayer Workshop

Families can struggle to find time for spiritual practices that fit the schedule of the comings and goings and the ages of the members. These suggestions can be offered during a summer program for children and parents, as a Saturday morning workshop, or over the course of several evenings. Information can be found in the entries for July 2–22. These suggestions cover some of the core practices for nurturing faith and prayer practices in the home.

Use the following questions to start conversations at the beginning of each session:

1. What are some of the ways your family currently prays?

2. What are the ways that the Bible and Bible stories are shared and present in the home? Are there Bibles and Bible storybooks for all ages? Any art or videos that you find helpful in talking about the Bible?

3. What are the ways your family could celebrate the church seasons? (Advent wreaths, Christmas trees, three kings, Lenten crosses, Easter eggs, and Pentecost doves are ideas that can get the discussion started.)

4. Talk about family graces, bedtime prayers, and blessing prayers in nature. Try writing or singing some prayers.

5. Involving children in caring for the earth and serving those in need is an active form of prayer. What are some ways your family can make a difference in your community or your world?

 # Meeting Openers

Church or other meetings can be rich times to focus participants' attention on some thought, issue, or concern. The prayers at the beginning of each month in *Openings* can provide seasonal prayers that encourage spiritual awareness of the changing of the seasons. Spring prayers lift up Easter and new life. Summer prayers turn to flowers, vacations, and renewal. Fall prayers focus on harvest, colors, and preparation for letting go. You may offer these prayers for the opening of meetings.

Another way to open meetings is by introducing participants to a saint or sage that may have particular relevance to the kind of meeting or issue at hand. Spiritual figures, social justice leaders, teachers, artists, and musicians are featured prominently in *Openings*. Pope Francis (May 5) could help focus on care for the poor. Rachel Carson (Sept. 22) could help start a conversation on recycling and care of the earth. If you have a particular person you are interested in sharing about, the Index of Saints, Sages, and Events will prove helpful to you.

A particular gift of *Openings* is the inclusion of saints and sages from other countries and faith practices beyond the normal assumption of Roman Catholic saints. At a meeting you may wish to introduce members to the richness of spiritual gifts from Muslims like Rumi (Oct. 17) or Hafez (Nov. 8), Buddhists like Thich Nhat Hanh (Oct. 11), or Jews like Abraham Joshua Heschel (Dec. 23) or Elie Wiesel (June 13).

A Discernment/
Clearness Group
Practice

The entries for October 3–28 have information for various discernment practices. Consider forming a group and introducing some of these practices, particularly the Quaker Clearness Committee. Invite participants of the group to take turns bringing a decision to the group so the group can ask questions that might reveal the desirable path. Group members can rotate serving as the focus person and the facilitator.

Rev. Larry J. Peacock, well known for his ability to help spiritual seekers find and celebrate the sacred in the everyday, is executive director of Rolling Ridge Retreat and Conference Center in North Andover, Massachusetts. He is also a spiritual director, retreat leader and speaker, and has taught at Boston University School of Theology. He has also served churches in Manchester, England, and in Michigan and California, including twenty years at Malibu United Methodist Church. For over thirty years, he has visited monasteries and retreat centers around the world, including Taizé in France, Iona in Scotland, a pilgrimage to Assisi in Italy and a sabbatical year at Pendle Hill, the Quaker study and contemplation center outside Philadelphia. He has been actively involved in the Academy for Spiritual Formation as a retreat leader, faculty presenter, writer and advisory board member.

PHOTO: ANNE BROYLES

Larry is the author of several books, including *Heart and Soul: A Guide to Spiritual Formation in the Local Church,* and many articles on spirituality and worship. He is married to author Anne Broyles; they have two children, two foreign exchange daughters and several pets.

Rev. Larry J. Peacock is available to speak to your group or at your event. For more information, please contact us at (802) 457-4000 or publicity@skylightpaths.com.

"A freshly prepared feast for the hungry heart.... Accessible to anyone—inside and outside gathered communities of faith—willing to pause for a few moments to be fully present to this particular day."
—**Alice Mann**, consultant, speaker; author, *Holy Conversations* and
The In-Between Church

"Simple yet wonderfully wise ponderings and prayer practices refresh the spiritual traveler and help to uncover the source of blessing hidden in each day."
—**Wendy M. Wright, PhD**, professor of theology,
John C. Kenefick Chair in the Humanities, Creighton University

"Sensibly down-to-earth ... will appeal to Christians of all denominations who want to stay alive to the Spirit one day at a time."
—**Wilkie Au, PhD**, associate professor,
Department of Theological Studies, Loyola Marymount University

Walking Together, Finding the Way®

SKYLIGHT PATHS®
PUBLISHING

Sunset Farm Offices, Route 4, P.O. Box 237
Woodstock, VT 05091
Tel: (802) 457-4000 Fax: (802) 457-4004

www.skylightpaths.com

Find us on Facebook®
Facebook is a registered
trademark of Facebook, Inc.

Insights and Ideas for Using *Openings* in Small Groups, Classes, Family Devotions and on Retreats, Including Models for:

- One- and Two-Day Retreats
- Classes on Prayer Practice and Writing Prayers
- Family Prayer Workshop
- Group Discernment Practice

About *Openings*, 2nd Edition: *A Daybook of Saints, Sages, Psalms and Prayer Practices*

This is a prayer book for every day of the year for people who don't usually think about using a prayer book. Drawing on a wide variety of resources—lives of saints and sages from every age, psalms, guides for personal reflection and suggestions for practice—Rev. Larry J. Peacock offers helpful guidance for anyone hungry for a richer prayer life. Each day's reading has four parts:

- Remember a notable person of faith or a significant event
- Read a psalm or another scripture passage
- Ponder that day's scripture or person of faith
- Practice a variety of different ways to pray, including prayer through play, music and physical movement

This new edition features the addition of ancient and modern sages from inside and outside the Christian tradition as well as updated resources for deepening your spiritual life throughout the year.

Praise for *Openings*, 2nd Edition: *A Daybook of Saints, Sages, Psalms and Prayer Practices*

"Lives up to its title.... Put the contents of this book into practice and it will hallow your daily life."

—**Parker J. Palmer**, author, *Healing the Heart of Democracy, Let Your Life Speak* and *A Hidden Wholeness*

"Enriched by the guidelines for use on retreats, in prayer groups, and for special occasions, and is very user friendly.... Creates a rhythm in the reader's soul, helping to establish a rule of life."

—**Rev. Jane E. Vennard**, spiritual director, retreat leader; author, *Fully Awake and Truly Alive: Spiritual Practices to Nurture Your Soul*

"Larry Peacock ... has poured his spiritual insight into the pages of this wise book."

—**Martin Sheen**

"Wonderfully helpful [and] wise.... No matter where you may be in your exploration of prayer and meditation, [this] is an excellent guide."

—**Rev. Dr. Ted Loder**, author, *Guerrillas of Grace*

Walking Together, Finding the Way®

SKYLIGHT PATHS® PUBLISHING

www.skylightpaths.com

$9.99 (Higher Outside the U.S.)
ISBN 978-1-59473-572-1

Printed in the USA
CPSIA information can be obtained
at www.ICGtesting.com
JSHW060056150824
68134JS00032B/2754

9 781594 735721